I see the Earth.
I am looking at Her and smile
Because She makes me happy.
The Earth, looking back at me
Is smiling too.
May I walk happily
And lightly
Upon Her.

Navajo Chant

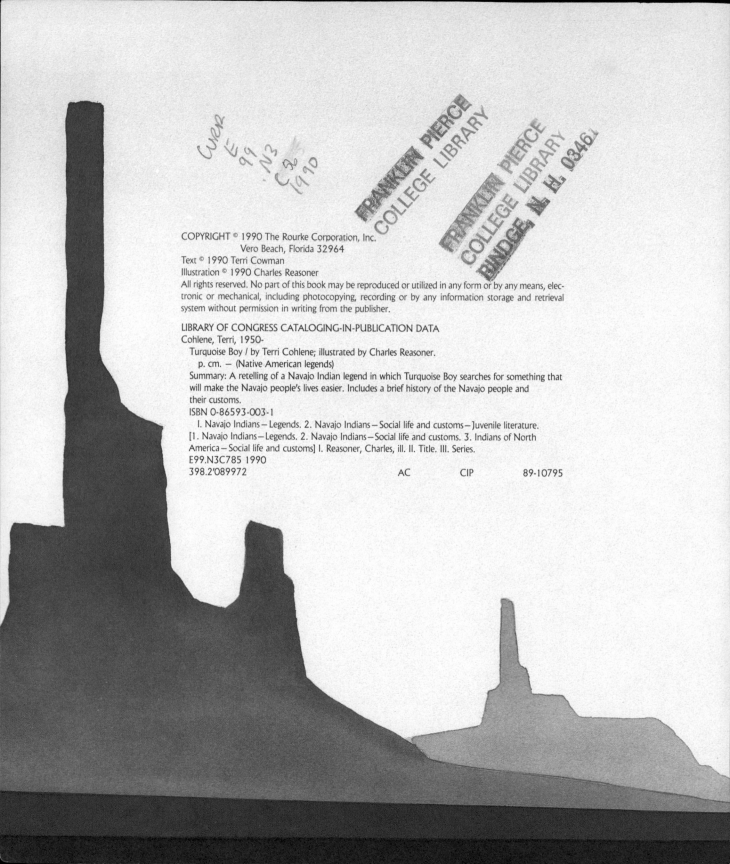

LIBRARY OF CONGRESS CATALOGING-IN-PUBLICATION DATA
Cohlene, Terri, 1950-
     Turquoise Boy / by Terri Cohlene; illustrated by Charles Reasoner.
        p. cm. — (Native American legends)
     Summary: A retelling of a Navajo Indian legend in which Turquoise Boy searches for something that will make the Navajo people's lives easier. Includes a brief history of the Navajo people and their customs.
     ISBN 0-86593-003-1
        I. Navajo Indians—Legends. 2. Navajo Indians—Social life and customs—Juvenile literature.
     [1. Navajo Indians—Legends. 2. Navajo Indians—Social life and customs. 3. Indians of North America—Social life and customs] I. Reasoner, Charles, ill. II. Title. III. Series.
     E99.N3C785 1990
     398.2'089972   AC   CIP   89-10795

Turquoise Boy

A NAVAJO LEGEND

WRITTEN AND ADAPTED BY TERRI COHLENE

ILLUSTRATED BY CHARLES REASONER

DESIGNED BY VIC WARREN

Watermill Press
Mahwah, N.J.

I n the days of long ago, when the Holy Ones still visited this land, a young Navajo named Turquoise Boy looked down on his people. In the heat of the desert, he saw them toil in their fields of corn and squash. He watched them labor under baskets heavy with fruit and nuts.

Turquoise Boy was saddened. My father, Sun Bearer, brings sunshine for the crops, but he offers little else. If only there were something I could do.

"Mother," he said, "The People work hard in their fields and search long in the desert for food. Surely there is something to make life easier for them?"

Changing Woman looked up from grinding her corn. "That may be so, my son. I am not certain."

"But you are mother of all people. Do you not wish for this also?"

Changing Woman resumed her grinding. "What you seek is not a simple thing," she said. "You must prove yourself worthy. Perhaps you would find the answer with the Talking Gods on the White Shell Mountain of the East."

"I will do as you say, Mother," said Turquoise Boy, and he set off at once.

5

Many days he walked before finally reaching a giant hogan. It was surrounded by baskets filled with white shells. The Talking Gods greeted him and asked the purpose of his visit.

"The People work hard in their fields and search long in the desert for food," he said. "Surely there is something to make their lives easier?"

The Talking Gods shook their heads. "What you seek is not ours to give. Take these white shells and go to our brothers of the sacred Turquoise Mountain. Perhaps they know the answer."

Turquoise Boy accepted their gift and turned his steps southward. Many suns had passed when he finally reached a giant hogan surrounded by baskets filled with turquoise stones.

He greeted the Holy Ones there and asked them his question. "The People work hard in their fields and search long in the desert for food. Surely there is something to make their lives easier?"

But the Talking Gods sent him away with only a basket of blue stones. "Perhaps our brothers of the Yellow Abalone Shell Mountain in the West know the answer," they said.

When Turquoise Boy arrived at the Holy Mountain of the West, the Talking Gods there said, "What you seek is not ours to give. Accept this basket of shells and visit our brothers on the Black Jet Mountain of the North. Perhaps they know the answer."

But the Talking Gods of the North did not give him the answer. "Take this basket of jet stones and return to your mother," they said. "Who would know better than Changing Woman?"

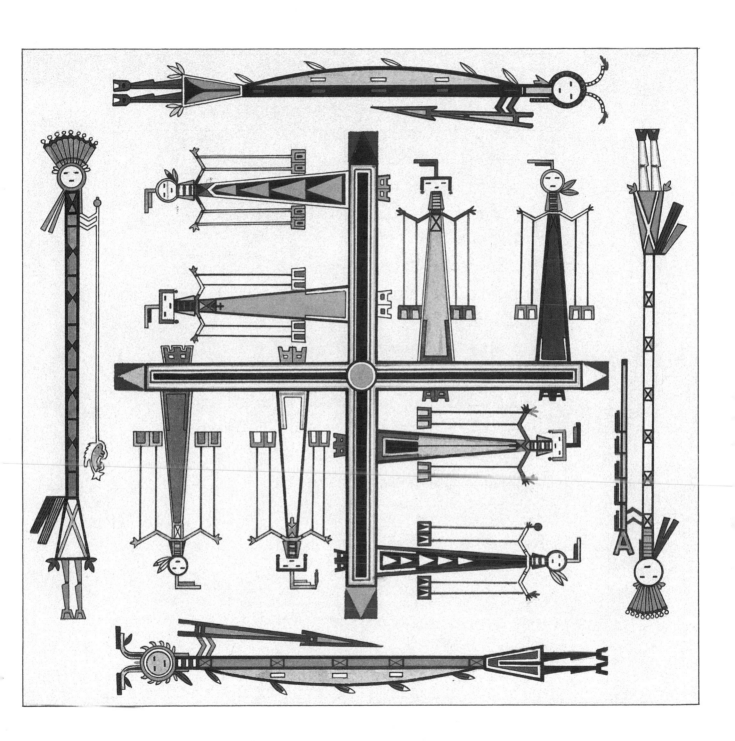

Turning his tired moccasins back to Dinetaa, Turquoise Boy carried home the baskets from the Talking Gods. "I have failed, Mother," he said. "I did not find a way to make life easier for The People. I bring only these gifts from the Talking Gods."

Changing Woman smiled. "You have done well, my son," she said.

"But, Mother," said Turquoise Boy, "I do not understand. The Talking Gods said *you* would know best how to make life easier for The People."

In answer, Changing Woman left her grinding stone and went inside her hogan. Soon she returned with a small pouch of soft deerskin. From each of the four baskets, she took a shell or stone and dropped it into the pouch. "Take this to your father," she said. "Surely he will see your worthiness."

Turquoise Boy tied the pouch to his belt and traveled toward Sun Bearer's home in the East. He saw rattlesnakes coiled in the sun and scorpions hurrying from one clump of sage to another.

The wind carried the scent of juniper, and Air Spirit whispered, "This is not an easy path. Perhaps you should turn back."

The young Navajo laughed. "I am not afraid, my friend. I have walked this path before. I have songs to protect me." Suddenly, fiery hot sands swirled up all around and cacti hurled their needles. Boulders from the cliffs above fell toward him.

Turquoise Boy chanted rhythmically,

"Beauty before me,
Beauty behind me,
Beauty above me and
Beauty beneath me."

At once, the sands settled into place, the cacti held their spears, and the rocks rolled harmlessly away.

Turquoise Boy sang as he walked on until finally, his path led across a rainbow bridge to Sun Bearer's great hogan. Hissing filled the air as snakes flicked their tongues at him. Strong winds tore at his hair and lightning bolts seared the sky.

But Turquoise Boy could not be frightened away. Just then, Sun Bearer stepped out from his lodging. He greeted the boy and asked the purpose of his visit.

"I bring greetings from Changing Woman, Father," said Turquoise Boy, handing him the pouch. "The People work hard in their fields and search long in the desert for food. Surely there is something to make their lives easier?"

Sun Bearer shook his head. "In what way, my son?"

Turquoise Boy thought of the many moons his search had taken him, and of his worn moccasins and sore feet. "Walking is slow and tiring," he said. "Perhaps there is a better way to get from place to place?"

Sun Bearer frowned. "I travel on sunbeams, rainbows and lightning. It is foolish to think mankind could do this." He gave back the deerskin pouch. "Return to your mother. It is time for my daily journey to the West."

With a heavy heart, Turquoise Boy once again walked the path homeward. As he crossed the Mountain-That-Is-Wide, he saw a ladder sticking up from a hole in the ground. "It was not here when I passed this way before," he said. "I have heard of a world below. Could this be the way to reach it?"

He looked down the hole and was startled to see an old fat man sitting at the foot of the ladder. "Is that one who walks the earth?" called the man.

"It is I, Turquoise Boy. Who are you?"

"I have been called many things, but you may call me Mirage Man. Come down so I can see you better."

Turquoise Boy descended the twelve rungs and stood in a wide cavern. The old man asked, "What is your purpose in traveling this path?"

"I seek a way to make life easier for The People."

Mirage Man saw the pouch hanging at the boy's belt. "You are the one I knew would come someday," he said. "Come. I will show you something."

He walked along a path until he came to a door facing east. He opened it, and Turquoise Boy gasped. In a white pollen mist, grazing on wildflowers, were magnificent creatures he had never seen before.

"These are Sun Bearer's horses," said Mirage Man. Then from Changing Woman's pouch, he took the white shell and placed it in a horse's mouth. Next, he removed it and returned it to the pouch together with pollen from the horse's mane.

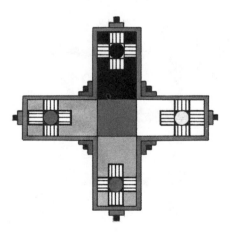

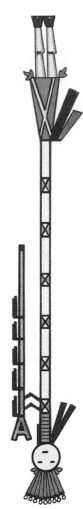

"Come," said Mirage Man, and he led the boy to the south meadow. There, a sky-colored horse rolled on the ground. Then it stood and shook off a cloud of glittering dust. Behind him, an entire turquoise herd pranced and neighed.

Mirage Man repeated his ceremony with the turquoise stone before showing the boy the yellow herd of the West and the black herd of the North. Each time, Mirage Man rolled the proper shell or stone in a horse's mouth and shook pollen from its mane.

Finally, Turquoise Boy said, "These animals would indeed make life easier for The People. How can we prove worthy of such a gift?"

Mirage Man was pleased with the question. "First you must learn to keep the horse sacred," he said, and he taught Turquoise Boy a holy song. "This you must remember and teach The People of Dinetaa." He handed back the pouch and said, "Go, now. Take this to Changing Woman."

Turquoise Boy returned home and found his mother weaving cloth outside the hogan. "I bring a song and a gift from Mirage Man," he said.

Changing Woman looked up and smiled. "You have indeed proven yourself worthy, my son." She took the pouch. "It is time," she said. "Send messengers to The People and the Holy Ones. Ask them to come while I go inside and prepare for the *hatal*."

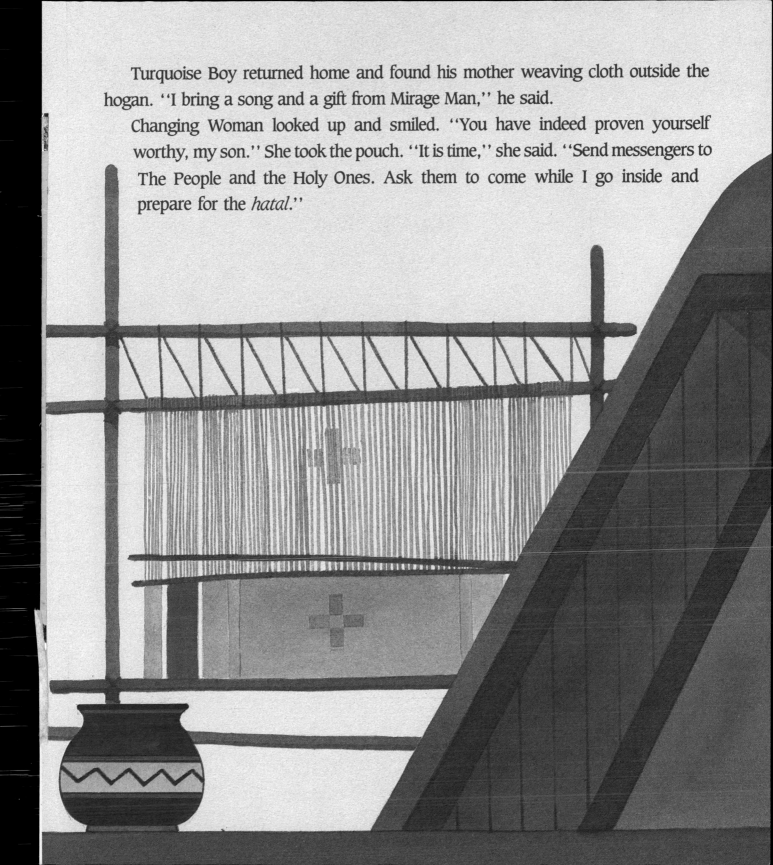

Turquoise Boy did as his mother asked, then went into the hogan to watch her. Changing Woman took a deerskin, spread it on the floor and put upon it the beads and shells from Mirage Man and the Talking Gods. Then she laid out ears of white corn, yellow corn, blue corn and corn-of-many-colors.

Over this, she sprinkled the sacred pollen. Finally, Changing Woman covered all she had done with twelve more skins. "I am ready," she said. "Now you must help me chant."

Outside, The People and Talking Gods had gathered. Moon was there, and Mirage Man and the Mist People. Sun Bearer joined them also. They built a fire and sat on the ground, chanting. They sang hogan songs, healing songs and songs of blessing. Turquoise Boy came out and taught them the song of the horse.

Into the night they sang. Until finally, Sun Bearer left for his daily journey. The God People nodded into sleep, and as they slept, Turquoise Boy closed his eyes tightly and sang for horses.

Suddenly, there was neighing under the deerskins as they trembled and began to rise. Then, with the first rays of the sun, came horses of white shell, turquoise, yellow abalone, and black jewel.

They rose up and kicked off their blankets, and as their numbers increased, the Navajo rejoiced. They rejoiced for their gift, and for Changing Woman, and for Turquoise Boy.

To this day, the people of Dinetaa offer pollen to the winds, and they chant for the sacred horse,

"*Nizho'ko ani-hiye!*
Nizho'ko ani-hiye!"
"How joyous he neighs!
How joyous he neighs!"

THE NAVAJO

Navajos lived in structures called hogans. Traditionally, the entrance was always on the east side, and the four main poles pointed north, east, south and west. There were three types of hogans:

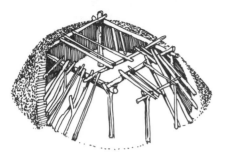

Four-sided leaning log hogan

Conical forked-pole hogan

Corbeled log roof hogan

UTAH   COLORADO

NEV.

JICARILLA
APACHE

N. TIWA

HAVASUPAI   NAVAJO   TEWA
        HOPI   KERESAN

JEMEZ TANO

WALAPAI   ZUNI LAGUNA S. TIWA

CAL.
MOJAVE   ARIZONA   ACOMA NEW MEXICO

YAVAPAI   PIRO
      WESTERN
      APACHE

CHIRICAHUA
     APACHE   MESCALERO
MARICOPA   APACHE

PAPAGO   PIMA

NAVAJO HOMELAND

They call their home "Dinetaa," meaning "land of The People." It's in the southwestern United States, an area of extreme contrasts: steep mesas, cold mountains, hot desert floor. Often, there wasn't enough water to raise good crops, and sometimes there was flash flooding.

They lived in small hogans, built apart from one another for privacy. These dome-shaped homes were made of wooden poles and sticks, and were often reinforced with mud or stones. They had one room, no windows, and a tunnel doorway.

The Navajo moved their homes to find wild food, good grazing lands and water. Because of this, they often had one hogan in the desert and one in the mountains.

The Navajo observed many ceremonies in which members wore masks and costumes representing gods and powerful beings.

Haschogan — The House God, a very kind and important god.

Haschebaad — Played by men, these female gods were often called upon to help heal the sick.

This silver "concha" belt is a fine example of Navajo jewelry.

NAVAJO PEOPLE

They called themselves "Dinneh," which means "The People." The word "Navajo" comes from the Pueblo word "Navahu," meaning "planters of huge fields."

They are the largest tribe in the United States. Related to the native people of Alaska and Canada, they moved into the area we now call Arizona and New Mexico between 800 and 1400 A.D.

The early Navajo made weapons from wood and stone and hunted small game such as birds, squirrels and rabbits. They raided nearby tribes for food, supplies and women. They also gathered wild nuts, bulbs, insects, grass seeds and cactus fruits to eat.

Zahadolzha — Known as the Fringe Mouth Gods, they made the first sand paintings.

Tobadzischini — Turquoise Boy's younger brother; one of twin sons of Changing Woman, the chief goddess of the Navajo.

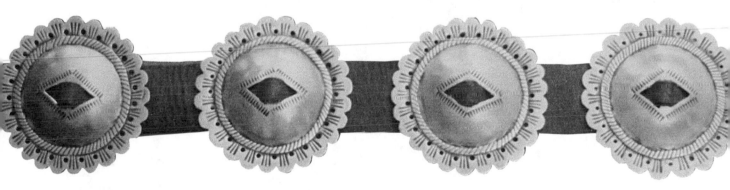

What clothing they wore was from rabbit skins or twisted fibers of the yucca plant. The men wore breechclouts and knee-high moccasins; the women wore skirts and sandals.

Eventually, the Navajo adjusted to their adopted home. They learned farming, pottery and weaving from the Pueblos, and silversmithing from the Mexicans. Even some of their religious ceremonies are similar to those of the neighboring tribes.

After the Spanish introduced horses and other livestock in the sixteenth century, the Navajo became primarily shepherds, tending flocks of goats and sheep, used for food and clothing.

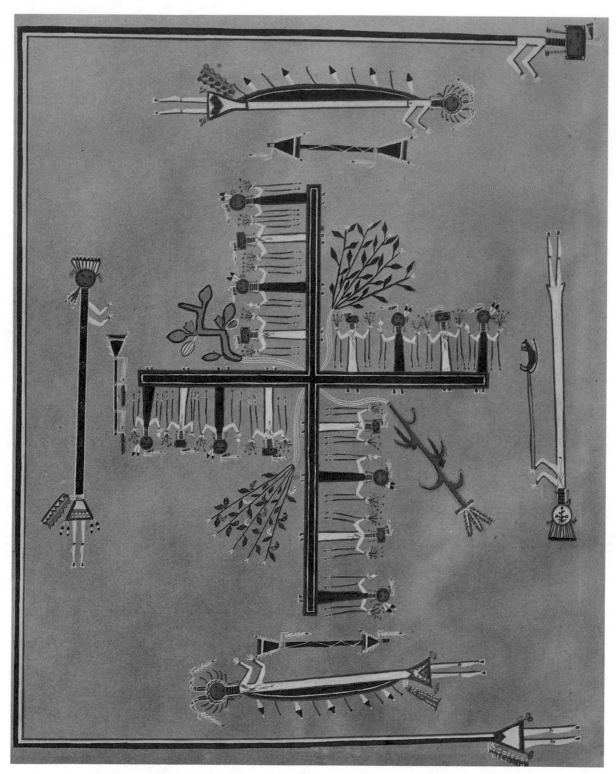

38

This 1904 photograph shows Hastobiga, a Navajo Hatali.

NAVAJO BELIEFS

Like all Native Americans, the Navajo are a very religious people. They believe the Holy Ones brought them to this World of White Brightness from four worlds below ours. They were taught to respect the spirits of all things and to protect the harmony of nature.

According to the elders, Dinetaa is held up by four sacred mountains, homes of the many gods who rule their universe. The most powerful god, Sun Bearer, and one of his wives, Changing Woman, created the Navajo race. Their sons, Turquoise Boy and his twin, were responsible for ridding the world of many evils.

Hatals, or chants, are the major Navajo celebrations. The Hatali, or medicine man, leads the sing and makes the appropriate offerings, such as sacred corn pollen sprinkled in the wind.

He may also create a sacred dry painting. This must be made after sunrise and destroyed before sundown, or made after sundown and destroyed before sunrise. Dry paintings are made in the earth and are pictures using pollen, powdered corn meal, colored sand, ground charcoal and minerals. Their purpose is to ensure healing, or rain, or safety, or beauty.

◁ This 1907 dry painting was used in a healing ritual. It shows singing gods seated upon two crossed logs which whirl around in a mythic lake. The light figures are female, the dark ones male. They sing about all life-giving plants, including the most important, which are pictured: corn, beans, squash and tobacco. After the ritual was finished, the painting was destroyed.

A Navajo Hatali prepares a sand painting to be used to heal a sick child.

NAVAJO TODAY

After signing a peace treaty, the Navajo moved to a thirteen-million-acre reservation. It's located in the ''Four Corners'' region where New Mexico, Arizona, Utah and Colorado intersect.

During World War II, the Navajo were heroes. Many served as radio men. Using their complex native language, they were able to send and receive top secret information without the enemy understanding the messages.

Today, many Navajo live in the traditional way, tending their flocks and practicing the old ways. Others have jobs in tourism, oil or other more modern careers. Even so, they still hold sacred many of the teachings of their elders.

Navajo women wove some of the world's most beautiful designs on looms like these. Often, their babies were propped nearby in their cradleboards.

This type of blanket design has a fitting name—Eye Dazzler.

IMPORTANT DATES

800-1400	Navajo arrive in Arizona, New Mexico area
1540's	Coronado explores the Southwest. Spanish introduce horses to Navajo
1853	Gadsden Purchase establishes southwest U.S. border
1862	Kit Carson leads "March of Death," sending Apache and Navajo to concentration camps
1868	Navajo reservation established

1872	Navajo teach silversmithing to the Zuni	1924	Native Americans born in U.S. declared citizens
1890	Battle of Wounded Knee, ending Major Indian Wars	1948	Arizona and New Mexico are last states to give Native Americans the right to vote
		1968	Indian Civil Rights Act gives Native Americans the right to govern themselves on reservations

This Navajo girl wears
a colorful blanket and
turquoise and silver jewelry.

GLOSSARY

Corn Pollen: A symbol of life

Dinetaa: Land of The People

Hatal: Chant ceremony often lasting days

Hogan: Dome-shaped lodge

Jet: Black substance, cannel coal

Mesa: High, flat table lands

Navajo: From Pueblo, "Navahu," meaning "planters of huge fields"

Pueblo: Neighboring tribes originating in Central America

Talking Gods: The Holy Ones

Turquoise: A precious blue stone; also a bluish-gray color, "A piece of the sky"

Some Navajo hogans were built in the shelter of canyons.

PHOTO CREDITS

Page 32: Monument Valley, photo courtesy of Arizona Office of Tourism.

Page 33: A Son of the Desert—Navaho, photo by Edward S. Curtis. Special Collections Division, University of Washington Libraries, neg. no. UW 11599.

Page 34: Navajo Women with Hogan, photo by P. Harrington. Colorado Historical Society, neg. no. F 15,887.

Page 36: Haschogan—Navaho (neg. no. UW 11600), Zahadolzha—Navaho (neg. no. UW 7300), Haschebaad—Navaho (neg. no. UW 11602), Tobadzischinl—Navaho (neg. no. UW 11603), all photos by Edward S. Curtis, 1904. Special Collections Division, University of Washington Libraries.

Silver Concha Belt, photo by Roy Rosen. Special Collections, University of New Mexico Library, neg. no. 000-477-0274.

Page 38: Shilhne'ohli—Navaho, photo by Edward S. Curtis. Special Collections Division, University of Washington Libraries.

Page 39: Hastobiga—Navaho Medicine-Man, photo by Edward S. Curtis, 1904. Special Collections Division, University of Washington Libraries, neg. no. UW 11598.

Sand Painting To Be Used To Heal Sick Child, photo by Boltin, 1954. American Museum of Natural History, neg. no. 2A 3634.

Page 40: Navajo Women and Looms. Peabody Museum, Harvard University, neg. no. N 29547.

Navajo Rug, Eye Dazzler. Stark Museum of Art, Orange, Texas, neg. no. 82.900/93.

Page 42: Navajo Shepherd with Flock, Monument Valley. Photo courtesy of Arizona Office of Tourism.

Page 44: Four Corners Navajo, photo by Roy Rosen. Special Collections, University of New Mexico Library, neg. no. 000-477-0521.

Page 45: Cañon Hogan—Navaho, photo by Edward S. Curtis. Special Collections Division, University of Washington Libraries, neg. no. UW 12928.

Page 47: Cañon de Chelly—Navaho, photo by Edward S. Curtis. Special Collections Division, University of Washington Libraries, neg. no. UW 10454.